Naked Light

poems for the spirit

Amanda North

BookLeaf
Publishing

India | USA | UK

Made with ❤ on the BookLeaf Publishing Platform
www.bookleafpub.in
www.bookleafpub.com

Dedication

For my past selves, who did they best they could with what they had. Life always finds a way to miracles, a lotus through the mud.

Preface

These poems are drafts of works from a larger project on grief, largely in the Japanese style of Zuihitsu poetic meditations. The more I meet myself on the page and guide others to meeting themselves, I find that a key to being able to live this life as fully as we can, is to embrace the constant undulations of grief. Grief is defined as the acute pain of loss. This loss can be literal, as in death, or more situational, like the end of a phase of life or relationship. Embracing life as change requires one to be an astute student of the process of moving through grief. Collectively and personally, this has been a decade of loss, these poems are my way of honoring all aspects of grief and allowing myself to move freely through: denial, bargaining, anger, depression, acceptance. I hope there are familiar moments in these words which speak to your heart, encouraging it to continue the brave process of breaking open.

Acknowledgements

In gratitude for all of my teachers, seen and unseen, thank you for finding your way to me.

This Is a Healing

a time to call forth all the gods:

the little ones in primrose
and the one holding sun
in their eye, a moon
as a single tooth,
and the garden inside their navel.

Sometimes we can't remember
how we knew them to be real,
now lodged in the gut
of our everyday meals and praise.

But here we are on our knees,
again, praying for rain to justify
yesterday's pain and last year's
rotten potato crops.

We are only called to sit down
at the dinner table, clean the dirt
off our knees to let that tender skin
render its form again. Then plate
the memory of our own face

glistened with sudden rain, creosote
filling the air, and eat our fill.

Seeking

Once, early mornings were natural,
an innocence of dew
lined grass. I would seek
the beings amongst the primrose
and those draped in the hair of willows.
It never occurred to question
their presence, from pages
of fairy-tales to the garden.

Their messages were little bells
in morning's stillness, bright
in their awakening, a clean slice
through silence: *you hold a key.*

Now, I work hard to rise
with the sun's eye and doubt
plagues my abilities to freely see,
an oddity of aging, the lack
of willingness to revelation.

In this moment, I watch
a yellow winged butterfly
trance through the marigolds,
a grace beyond any dancer,

the subtle simplicity of her wisping
through wind, blossom to blossom.

Between her dance is the key,
I whisper, as a lizard scurries
behind rosemary. It is a miracle
to be alive on these mornings,
despite an aged resistance.
As winter is soon to wipe sleep
over this land, my hope is to seek
out the little gods below decayed leaves
or wherever they may be hiding,
to remember all, even death, holds purpose.

Some ask how I submit myself
to the mysteries, the answer is simple:
I try to return to the curious sight
of my childhood, when time moved
as molasses and believing was obvious.

For the Self found in Death

As the earth turned her flesh to fire, our lungs started to drown. Isn't this the great irony, fire and water at opposite ends of the room, teasing each other of the time they once danced as lovers? I have been told to keep my body and breath steps away from any other and it is in this seclusion that I dream the most deeply about passion and what it is to feel another's hand rest on my lower back. Is all love found in this liminal space of desire and fear? That tension is what compels us to continue to create life. In my dreams, you touch me and your fingers are matches, but my stomach is an ocean. We meet at the most beautiful of spaces. Somehow, ivy grows from our feet. We wrap ourselves around the bedposts, cover corners of the room, shadows disappear as smoke, and we never wonder what happened outside the windows, while fire and water threaten to embrace, once again.

———

We put those that we cherished in carved wood or porcelain. It makes me want to escape, to pretend this all, life and love and death, were only strange prequel to the real start, a slow dream, the kind you regret to wake from. The sky lit on fire again tonight, but it did not mean you would come home. If the house were an ocean, you were the deck of a ship, and now I am left to the lacking mercy of the wind and sea. I'll sleep and sleep, imagine you free.

———

It seems as though the cicadas only wept during the sunlight until one night, as summer found his end in the cessation of fire. The silence was a sudden burden. I felt the cool of fall hinting at her arrival, a soft romance in the blue hours of morning or a gust slithering through the open window. This cry was not like that of the screech owl nesting in the tree next to my bedroom window, a wail that took its' nails against your bones. No, the cicada's cry was one of desire, a hum so low that only the skin on the back of your neck can sense it. Isn't this what we all hope for, a desire so primal, that we wish to molt our skin to find another body? Yet in the transient process of shedding to finding, those few moments hanging in the air before a storm, is where all the damage will be done, the vulnerable heart without a refuge.

———

We begin to prepare for the dead, their bodies and the questions while the air is filled with fumes of loss. *I'll organize the containers*, in flames or ice. You know this is when we all decide on a final rest for the bones that helped Spirit move through time on earth. Each delicate joint is tired from running or pivoting. Those that looked into my eyes, deeply during love, will turn away from my loss, struggling to witness my cooling skin. We try to decide the language we will organize for the children: books we will share and ancients' songs on the return to nonmaterial. The preparation is all self, missing final moments when their breath pulses in and out the ether, those last hours when they are a part of the collective rather than the eternal, returning home after the long, long journey.

———

You will feel alone for a long time. You will isolate your body in the way your mind urges. Life will seem at a standstill, moments slowly slipping like honey from a spoon. You will tell yourself that this will be forever, that this emptiness has taken over your body and you are now just a host for eternal longing. Until, one morning you will wake with the first hint of the sun out of her sleep, instinctively. You will be aligned with a time you had forgotten. Your skin will call your bones to move to the window, burst it open, and let in all the light you had denied existed. Your lungs will cry out to the blue line between the ocean and horizon that you are alive, truly alive and *here*. It will be an ancient language, one of the beings that came long before you, one that can only be known after transitions. As the sun reaches her peak above the clouds, your laughter will peel open bright as a blood orange, filling silence with the same curiosity of your most celebrated childhood. It is only then that you will know that grief finally found a room in which to rest, inside of you, and that you will carry the lost with you for the rest of your days in this unique body, until finally another great love will start to carry you.

Mask of the Divine: an elegy

Spirit flutters through
the cracked window-sill,
a shadow laced into slivers
of dawn's glow,
exhausted from its night-shapes
of a dandelion in a barrel,
two dragonflies suspended
over a river's muddied belly,
a crocus rupturing through
the garden bed, a blue angelfish
hook-sown on a wooden deck
breaking free
into water again——

                     salmon sunlight   drapes
over
               our   body   like a silk
gown   as you   crawl
               out of the glass
reflection
               and into our   bed
          humming   distant
harmonies   to awaken
            us   vertebrae   by

vertebrae   you have

                                   returned to us
                    gitana soul   as
captured wind

Lotus

Oh the singular truth of loving a dying thing, a being so close to the door of *next*, a body flailing in final attempts at being-ness.

We all reluctantly arrive in this valley of knowing, which all must pass through to the next adventure of so many names.

I've watched a comet, thousands and thousands of years old, climb the sky each night this week, looking to its slow effacement as I wait for you to find a comfortable contortion for sleep.

Can you see it, a question foolish in how lost it is to a past in which you could still see more than just nearby shadowed outlines.

As memories of me and my name have slowly erased themselves from your mind, we are creating a saint-like testimony to a church of non-being.

This process reminds me how small a part we play in the weaving web of the world, a tiny fiber of a singular string among millions.

It is not my stories that matter, or yours, it is something else beyond the limits of language and these aging bodies.

I want to know if there is an unspeakable wisdom that comes to us as we reach this transition, one we all will enter, not just witness while care-giving.

Will we understand mechanics of time or the root of fear or perhaps how many gods there really are looming over and around us in the cosmos?

Oddly, the last time we were at such a unique threshold was our childhood, so willing to share the unfathomable wisdoms of the great beyond of which we just entered from, a place of the ancestors and untold mysteries.

As we approach the other end of this lifetime, we tend to be mum mouthed of what we are starting to see of the other side, lock jawed to not be seen as pitifully strange.

A dying thing speaking the truth of the veil is marked as a delirium of sorts, something unsettled, where a child is marked curious and comical.

How do we end up coming to these conclusions?

You've taught me the strangeness of bodies connecting in the most non sensual of spaces, to look at the truth of the limitations of this flesh and still nurture.

How long do we deny the raw truth of these bodies, deny their requests of non-beautiful things, push them to their extinction, yet act surprised when we arrive at the humble gate of relying on other's bodies for basic function?

I am not sure if loving a dying thing will reveal all the knowledge I seek in this life, but I do know I have learned the singular truth of Love, in its strange muddy belly below the potential of any pink petals.

Siren: the first touch

If the ocean can swallow
a wave in a single

moment or the horizon
a setting star in the blink
of an eye, then how far

can two people escape
inside of each other's bodies,
a refuge of desire, joined

with the sweat of sudden want?

I can commit myself
to an ancient cause,
like raindrops to the sea,
if I feel it deep inside
my Bones, just as Atargatis
promised herself to water
after her groom died. Grief
can trace over flesh like scales,
with a languid glimmer,
& thrust in the neck as gills
for solemn sighs below the shore.

The punishment for loss
is a physical change,
to mark the murder
of a dying devotion, the willing rebuke
of years now confined to only memories.

In these times
words have little meaning,
less than a soul crying

out to join itself
to another--*there is*

some dawn in you
that I crave, I want
your guiding southern
cross inside of me:

You found me, curled
on a beach, legs unsteady.

As I tried to find
a serpent in a
a bottle of tequila,

my toes could not help
but find the shoreline,

waves beckoning me.
I fell towards you,
despite consciousness

warning my limbs
of the previous pain
from undertow's grasp.

It was only
a smile, beyond any
legend, like a butterfly
instinctively drinks
the tears of a turtle
to survive. How can I

write of these
ecstatic moments, how can one

promised in shame
to a life in the ocean
ever come back to dry land,
ever return to love again?

Sometimes, it is only
the hand of a stranger
made sudden betrothed,

his timber mast in a storm,
that can guide you home,
following the map of constellations
of the celestial glow
you held too deep
inside of yourself.

A Ghazal for Unraveling

Love vanished into the fog as winter shifted to spring, the air held a spell.
I reached for him & found nothing. When I reached again, I found myself.

As if I was only a basket waiting to be filled, he used to gift me
oranges & murmurs of *soon*. Like a wild Fire, I too became lost inside of myself.

A large swarm of locusts descended on a desert at sunset & I wept
when I imagined a great body of sand in shadow, the abrupt loss of identity.

My mouth settled on his chest, chin to sternum, a chant poured from my lips:
your eyes are absent lakes in winter, my stomach a ripe fruit you'll carve for yourself.

*Somedays, he would disperse as a hollow paper bag to a sudden breeze, a mere
shade of something once whole: a partnering in which I had once hoped to find myself.*

*A monk asked that I begin to practice peeling away
layers, as if I was
only yarn to untangle from the clumsy packaging of self
& mine.*

*Devastation will always flood my heart when a knife
makes its first cut,
or as desire disperses to a plague, or once the Sun
beckons: child, run back to yourself.*

Some People Smirk When I Say I'm a Poet

for my friend, Lulu

I think poetry can save our life.

So I hope this saves yours, or at least saves you some time:
Don't wait to remember that every morning is a miracle (*give me a few more lines, you cynics...*).
Seriously a miracle that you've woken up, again.
Don't wait to remember this until someone you love dies unexpectedly.

Like: you wake up and thoughtlessly rush to your task list and complain about feeling *tired*.
Thinking it's a day just like any other, because days are "endless."
Then you get this call, it's so absurd you almost laugh, "She's dead."
No, she isn't that is ridiculous, you think. *I just spoke with her, oh my god when did I last speak to her, her media must have been hacked, it can't be real, right?, why didn't I call her yesterday when I thought to, oh my god...*

It's taken me months, and even now I don't always remember, to believe one of my best friends took her life. I am not sure I'll ever know shock like that again. Or maybe I will, but I am more prepared for it now with the burden of experience.

It often takes humans experiencing extraordinary pain to remember that this life is a gift, a pure bizarre miracle, to be here, right now. Together, even in this poem.

Consider it: This rock spinning in a gargantuan galaxy, around other weird rocks, yet this one we can breathe on and it has sunsets that dissolve into a blue ocean every single day.

And somehow your parents met on this rock and connected, to make you, on purpose or accident, *who cares*, but so many moments coincided to bring you here. I learned that the theory is that it takes two and a half million people connecting for you to be even be born. Two and a half million first kisses that went really damn well. I mean how many first kisses are that good?

Then you continue to wake up, breathing this breathable air on this spinning rock and they even tell us that the same material that makes the shine in the stars that glitter over the night sky are in our teeth. Truly bizarre.

And we somehow meet other soul-friends here that we connect with instantly and share endless hours of conversation over Tupac's poetry and good food good wine and how to grow gardens in Texas heat and ofrendas and the magic of Dumbledore's knowing smile and how to make the world a more kind place.

Somehow this person is here at the same time as me on this spinning rock in the midst of shinning stars. We're both here and light sparklers on new years eve together, outside at midnight in our pretty dresses, laughing about shivering and our chattering star teeth, our skin littered with goosebumps.

Then she dies, but I still woke up that morning. I wish I could tell her what I learned today, that a swarm of ladybugs are called *loveliest*.

Do you understand now?
Please don't be like me and wait to believe all of this from experience.
Poetry can save us, if we'd only listen.

A Red Dress

Tattered at the knees, pockets pushing past the corner, hints of skin or underwear depending on the day.
These are the jeans where my feminine thrives, these are the jeans I pulled out of the trashcan as a teen when my mom threw them out for being so broken in and 'nasty'.
Levi tag faded, denim making way for light in the center, fabric softening to velvet.
Baggy, comfortable for work and movement, sitting on the floor, but hugging just so on my hip, curving with my ass.

These are the jeans I know you turn to look, they call you to your wild.
They call you to your celebrated childhood, they call you to a certain innocence.
A reminder that life is a purely sensual experience.

The bottom of the leg torn from boots, those nights dancing in a sequin top.
The side muddied from the garden, chlorophyll stained at a hem.
Some splatter on the thigh from feeding my lover last nights dinner, made from the garden to my stove top.

I can work beside you in these jeans, I'll help carry your furniture out of that loser's house when you finally listen to me to 'dump him', that you're too wonderful for crying over leftovers.

I can dance at a moments notice, drop it to the floor like my knees are still sixteen and the beat hits just right when to deny it would be to deny myself, never again.

I can crawl on the floor, meditate and pray, and writhe in my divinity when I feel the call, the wisp of wind along my collar bone, the hum of nature and silence, the smell of god in the air.

I'll get buried in these blue jeans, with the same voices of my life whispering "can you believe she would chose to do this for her funeral, how obscene, how bizarre."

My husband will tear these jeans off one afternoon after we plant a new tree, and place a seed in my womb so I'll carry new life, then I'll wear them unbuttoned and tight to the hospital to give birth.

I'll present to a room full of hundreds of women begging me to use language to give them the permission slip to pack light and move on to their new wild life, they won't know if they love me or hate me or want me to be their new lover, these jeans are just that fucking good.

I can promise you, in these jeans, I will make you feel, I will make you remember, you've got one shot at this

thing and its not the dress rehearsal, meet me on stage, just try to outshine me, but please just shine.
Lets dance and pray and garden and love through this entire weird journey to the other side.

In these jeans I'm more than a 90s model in a Pepsi cola commercial, I'm the goddamned sky.

October in Ireland

The way that media creates the space for paper cuts, dozens and dozens until you're left to bleed out. A mentor calls it *death by a thousand paper cuts.* I read somewhere that we were meant to only take in the information we take in a day in a lifetime.

How much are we drowning in the excess of *too much*?

Somedays I can hardly manage to call my own mother, so tired from all the falsehoods of connections and the burden of knowledge of traumas in countries I'll never visit or know the history. But I've seen a young mother there, her face wrecked with the lines of inequity and bombs. Next is a video of an influencer explaining *baby tox.* Drowning.

Is this all sustainable? I go for a small walk under the sun and feel the imbalance to my bones.

I knew you made him a playlist with a song titled something about falling in love in October. He took me out for my birthday that month, declared to the table that I was the love of his life, perfect in every way, so good to my core that it felt too much for him sometimes.

There is information like this which my heart will never make sense of. My head might be able to compartmentalize, but a heart doesn't. If I were your friend, what would you tell me to do with all this information?

I have always loved my birthday season, the seasonal shift and the subtle between of the weather. I have never been an extreme person. Anytime I try to wear those masks, I break. I break big, cracks through my center of gravity.

I remember seeing that playlist and cracking, thinking October were lost to me forever. Like the time I learned about him 'falling for' someone else while touring in Ireland. It was less about him and her, it was more about Ireland. Would it be lost to me forever? The country that I came home to in my late twenties, the country that was a the physical state of my soul? Was it tainted now with a memory I did not want?

It was less about you or her, less about him and me, more about October and Ireland. About too many contradictory memories associated with things I wanted a single love for—my birthday celebrations while the leaves change and a green in hue I had never seen in this lifetime.

Death by that many paper cuts can't be what life is all meant to be. I hope whoever reads this can stop justifying the paper cuts, walk away before you lose your Octobers and Irelands.

Undulations: Zuihitsu Grief Meditations

If death were just an hour and love a minute, which might I chose? Some may quickly claim love, despite the lack. Some may pretend that the deep song doesn't find them at night, a low hum of a birds' call or a slight whistle between branches to bring them home. I am more familiar with death, the slow effacement of my skin to the wind's hand. I have been walking this journey since the moment of my birth, where I shifted from becoming to erasing, slowly, but trying ever so hard to stay put. I have held a body in my arms, pressed against my chest, as life erased itself fully. It felt like sleeping, just as they say. But what you are not told is stun of silence, the laboring breath suddenly gone or the slight reverberation of the heartbeat that you knew to be commonplace, so that your hands ignored the sensation, disappeared. Once gone, that silence will take you to the core of the earth, seeking that deep song to curse it and wish the idea of you being born was only as fleeting as that last, sudden, inhale.

Kotadama

Give me a god who sings *yes,* a god who gifts the wild,
not corners or all sun,
a god of shadows and splendor, a god to define and
illuminate.

Give me a god who ebbs, as foaming surf, with the moon
and calls all
bodies divine while wrestling my mind in dirt and
laughter.

This god loves silence as equal as a barbaric yawp lost
to an endless sky blushed in sunset.

This god calls forth all beings to create a world that
mimics
cosmos, stars littered over navy bodies, wild wisps of
milk and clouds.

Give us a god holding a dandelion mid-wish, the
gossamer wing
of a sea-dragon, a balance for the thunder moan of *now*:

a god of more *yes* than *no*, more *and* than *or*, more
possible than defined,

a big god with many little gods in their fingertips, a
universe in their brow,

a god gifting all moon with sun, all
wild, all me, all wild.

Collective Nouns

A swarm of egrets is called a congregation. I learn
this after I see hundreds of egrets on my birthday.
Each year, on this day, some group of beings
appears to me, last year it was bees: a hive.

If there were a way to be a part of the loveliest
congregation, I would join, tether myself
to ideologies. Yet most human swarms
are just that, swarms. We rarely move
in beautiful unison towards a singular
ideal which could benefit the whole.

As the egrets circled the farm fields,
a sudden dip to a rise disappearing
in the beams of the sun, they eventually
staggered softly amongst two Oaks,
each branch holding dozens of angular bodies.

If I am to seek meaning, as a poet would,
there is no certainty to take from their graceful
endeavor, an artful collection in an ancient tree.

This year I am left, only, with a question to live into:

Is beauty in loss of self to a collective
or melancholy in the sudden departure of flying?

Miracle

for Saint Francis of Assisi & Charles Teitsworth

I prefer the bursting white flowers
    of early spring

to the raw green of summer.
    The honesty of a new bud

from the depths of winter's shadow,
    which conceals all change, all growth.

Beneath the sprawling limbs,
    naked, barren, to then suddenly

    remind us, one warmer morning,
that under the dew

    newness waited, patient, despite
the cold rejection of the sun.

    Life is still,
always, brimming.

Rumination VI

The morning sang in subtle
hums and moans, an engine
idled in a driveway, a wren
declaring the shift from dawn,
as I found a little god
in a cup of tea.
Are gods of this size only
an idea, a lip curled back
from heat? Sometimes I wish
for the past to change
or the future to mold, yet
neither are neither.

——

Would some claim the cosmos
born of its navel and desire it
to judge a spirits' ability to float
or burn? This daemon may never
win a war or take flight as a falling
star, but could it bring the past
or the future meet my desires?

Rumination XIII

What if I stood up, flesh
first and pushed into the altar
to make it smell
of my sweat and need?
What if I fell
into that ritual, danced on
the velvet covering dead
trees and crushed it to a color
I find inside my body,
if I sang new notes into this sad
song and cried out of the stars
in my teeth, shining one by one
as I crush an offering in my jaw?

Aren't we all gods inside?
We eat them all the time.

—

I once found the almighty
in a beetle. Its dead
body offered up
as an emerald to the sky
and I thought--*Spirit, why do you
put your beauty in such*

tiny splendor––before I lifted
my foot from the crunch. God
gave me those glinted wings
and I fastened them around
my neck so my voice could fly
faster up the wind for my prayers
to hang on clear threads
before the heavenly altars and organ.

Later, as I drank
water, angels filtered down
my throat to feed
my cells, two by two.

——

I deserve this offering and altar
only in a way that my body
calls, don't you understand?
This is where it all becomes one:
these different worlds, condemnations,
incense, and cut star-fruit dripping
down the offering plate.
All inside of me, of us,
the universe in my mouth
and celestial bodies in my eyes,
a reminder of the infinite: truths.

——

What if I raised my hands to the dark
night sky and cried out--
I am here?

Moksha

The desert has no memory. Sun beats
on its chest, collarbone glistens: I wait
for rain, an angry sea filling the sky
to break, blow, burn, make a new world order.
Agave pierces clouds while amethyst
mountains rest in heavy sleep. I have asked
permission to make this desolate ground
my home. Beneath these imagined oceans,
are forgotten idols. There is a thirst
that causes some to drown, doubting the sky
will open again. Like the desert, I
must look to the sky and expect nothing
in return, while watching angels fly through
stars to the embers of a rising sun.

Inca Doves

Is it odd to say I thought of you
as I pulled a dead dove from

the swimming pool? Spine up
to God, floating lightly with

its bright beak face down.
Streams of red outlined

the strange sight. I gently scooped
him up, ignorant of *sex*, his eyes

closed so gently as if in prayer.
His only mate's claws licked the fence,

like little tongues, as she watched on.
Wings magnificently stiff and his feet

frayed wide in la petite mort. You came
to mind. His neck was limp

as a cypress flower.
I had to look away

when his head snapped backward
while I laid him in spring grass.

November, 1

To love a dying
thing the size of my country
seems too much to bear.

An Auspicious Morning

"God breaks the heart again and again until it stays open"
How many hearts have I broken and how often will mine break? This is the wealth in which I wish to acquire in this lifetime:
a record number of times in which a single heart can break yet continue to live.

I lived so long with my heart guarded by walls, then I would let my heart stretch like a balloon but only to its edges.
That is it, isn't it, my consciousness was limited, restricted, suffocating.
Maybe the goal of all the work, the healing and the prayer, is that I allow my heart to break wide open with every tragic poem and photograph, not only at death of a friend or the loss of love.
I hope that I am wise enough to look at the world and love it as big as I possibly can.
Which is to say the world will tragically break my heart as many times as it provides me a miracle. This is gravity.
Miracles can be as small as a green beetle landing on your hand so peacefully as you harvest the tomatoes or

as large as the sudden gift of having your home blessed by Tibetan monks one rainy morning in fall.

Heartbreak can be small or shattering, as well. The glance of a loved one which reflects the aging in their eyes and you allow your heart to feel the truth of impermanence, that this place will the the one you remember the moment they are no longer on this earth. Heartbreak can also be witnessing the gravity of war on innocence, allowing yourself to truly see the violence which took sixteen thousand four hundred and fifty six children in a single year. You watch the mother's tears push through her dirt stained cheeks, you feel your heart shatter as the tear becomes your own.

It is here that our hearts grow to new dimensions. By allowing in the heartbreak, we have allowed in God, acquired clearer eyes to see miracles, clearer eyes to see that there is no separation between *me* and *you*.

Stigmata

I have been told, by labored lectures and the passing of a spring evening through newly blossomed branches, that we waste our suffering.

I cannot decide if I like the feeling of grass under my feet or if I prefer the blister of sun soaked sand, there is something clean about the pain, but I cannot tell this to a creator who opens skies to wash all to mud.

We need the spring to court summer and we need fall to warn crops of winter's wrath, but I have stood in a rotting field and I am not sure if there is any wisdom that can prepare your heart for certain pain.

Many days, I am asked to use my mind to explain histories, ancestors' histories that cannot be my own, but eyes look to me with the same desire of a whale approaching a school of krill, and I give in to speak truths I may never believe.

I want you to know that I have tried, spent life in movement partnered to breathlessness, from prayer to reaching, finger by finger, into a god's open wound.

There are many dances I have learned, my legs contorted and arms bracing the air for the inquisitive gaze of an audience.

Yet each night, just before my body releases my spirit to waltz through the constellations, I resist.

Despite my daily penance to listen to the elders' call of impermanence, despite my attentive reading of all the prophet's poems, or nodding to strangers as I hold hands with heartbreak, I still resist.

One truth that reappears season after season and page after page is that all will suffer, otherwise choice dissipates as dew, and I only wish for the wide wings of a blue- heron not yet those of an angel.

With this, I yearn to drift into dreams freely as a dog, enjoy the wisp of my soul slipping away to expand through Western wind in the navy sky, until I trap her again, come sunrise.

Bloodline

The loneliest feeling, she said on a day
when the sky was clear, *is watching an airplane
fly away,*

and in the middle of Valentine Texas
a single machine mends
railroad tracks,
cracks splinter form

while buzzards string
red remains over gravel lanes.

Before, she created still-life with oil paint
and after she drank while wrinkles set.

The horizon is only purple mountains and lone
windmills, when desolation surrounds
will it eventually
entrap?

A pecan orchard sits heavy on this desert land,
if it is pollution that makes the sky
shades of pink
then I want that inside my lungs.

All dirt trails branch like veins into strangers
homes. We will finish alone.
If creeks ever existed atop this sand
then each left with the Mexican wolves.

Her spine fell westward
with her mind
and she forgot our names,
we try to reconcile our anger.

Cacti survive droughts
then burst fuchsia flowers,
what a hope,
could anyone do any better?

November, 2

for Ruby

I am trying to be brave at Autumn's door
to winter, a willing walk through
the golden hues to a fresh bitter sting,
the long darkness. There is wisdom
there, in the next evolution. I know this,
but each time I am called forward
to a new season I resist. Don't we all
wish we could be bravest at thresholds?